ARRANGING

DECK

CHAIRS

ON THE

TITANIC

RABBIT HOUSE PRESS

Versailles, KY 40383

Copyright © 2020 by Mike Wilson

For inquiries about author appearances and orders, please visit www.rabbithousepress.com.

Front cover photo: Unknown photographer, [Anna Pavlova on board, arrives in Sydney from Queensland where her tour began in Townsville]. ca. 1929, photograph, State Library of New South Wales.

Back cover photo: Unknown photographer, [Titanic in Southampton], ca. 10 April 1912, photograph, https://commons.wikimedia.org/wiki/File:Titanic_in_Southampton.jpg (accessed May 1, 2020).

Editor: Erin Chander
Cover & interior design/formatting: Brooke Lee

Published in the United States by Rabbit House Press
Printed in the United States of America

ISBN: 978-1-7351727-0-5

Poems previously published:

45 Poems of Protest : "Constitutional Crisis"

Cagibi Literary Journal: "Hope"

"Measure for Measure"

Evening Street Review: "November 2, 2018"

killjoylit : "Breaking News"

The London Reader: "Howl"

"Happy New Year from Fox & Friends"

Ocotillo Review: "Thumbs Up"

This book is dedicated to those infected with the post-truth virus
and those who search for a cure.

Contents

ARRANGING

DECK

CHAIRS

ON THE

TITANIC

MIKE WILSON

Thumbs Up

(a golden shovel poem after Arthur Sze)

He swaggers through china shops smashing
mirrors and manners with a
jack-hammer hatred worn as jewelry.

He hurls parades of hand grenades in case
someone thinks he's not strong, grinning with
used-car salesman sincerity and shuffling a

pack of lies, sharpening the hatchet
for our collective suicide while he
sizes up suckers and grabs

whatever he can reach, stringing a
crime spree into a necklace
of notches in a gun. Sent from

Hollywood Heaven is what the
preachers say, discernment splintered
in prisms of stained glass.

Tiki torches and stone-cold faces and
riots in rubble as everyone races
to hiding places that shape-shift into

seats on a train to oblivion.

Patriarchy's Subtext

June and moon, love and above,
we roll these words like marbles under
your feet and you slip and fall

in our arms and we carry you off to
the dungeon where you satisfy our
needs and breed, so smile – or stamp

your tiny foot if you want – it's
not our fault you were born with a
hole and all those other grabbable

parts in America where little boys
fantasize with greedy eyes that
they are meant to be President.

Drinking Bleach

He's pushing his grocery cart toward me
Hot Pockets, Cheetos, a twelve-pack of beer

pasty-faced and prematurely
balding with a bushy beard

to compensate, frowning like someone
tricked him into eating a pickle

he's literally wearing a frigging
gun holstered at his waist

going-to-Publix-packing-heat gun
daring-someone-to-pull-on-me gun

twelve feet away his trigger's cocked
awaiting the President's tweet declaring

open season on liberals (finally!)
and here I am, a big fat squirrel

a deer in headlights wearing a shirt
Trump for Prison and looking like

an immigrant gay Nancy Pelosi
incarnation of what needs to be

killed, gutted and strapped across
the hood like an offering on the altar.

I tighten my bandana, shut the trunk
too late, he's in my face and says

Ditch the mask – the President opened America.
Some things even a sip of Clorox can't kill.

Putin's America

breathes in screen shots by offshore bots
texting diddled lines designed by script doctors
to infect us with dementia in which

                                       doom

is faceless fog   snow-blind eyes
                  don't see   ·

white coats lace straightjackets
red eyes band Ben Franklins
black helmets aim assault rifles

Breitbart pounds every door
Senators are frightened whores
democracy is melting

The Trump-Pence Blues
(to be performed in the manner of Bob Dylan's
"Leopard-Skin Pillbox Hat")

Donald Trump is wearing his
Make America Great Again
hat (....) (....) yeah
Swearing and a' wearing his
Make America Great Again
hat. (....) (....) Does it
make your twitter tweet when your
head is under something like
that? (....) (....) Gonna

build a big wall, now
down by the old Rio
Grande. (....) (....) Gonna
build a nice white wall
down by the old Rio
Grande. (....) (....) Gonna
truck us in some Mexicans
build it nice and tall with brown
hands. (....) (....) ohh

Got a problem, snowflakes? Just
ask the NRA to give you a
gun. (....) (....) Yeah
homeroom teachers are packing heat
even the lunch lady's carrying
one. (....) (....) If you
happen to run into Jesus, tell him
still ain't no place safe for him to
come. (....) (....) Mister

Pence is up in Frisco, he don't
need Kalashnikov to lock and
load (....) (....) Mister
Pence is up in Frisco, he don't
need no Kalashnikov to lock and
load (....) (....) He's waving his
Bible in your bedroom and
conversion therapy e-lec -
trodes! (....) (....) ohh

Football players dissing, singing
Mr. Francis Scott out-of-
Key. (....) (....) 'stead of
waving and parading all the
quarterbacks are dropping to their
knees.(....) (....) See the

10

blue lights flash in Ferguson?
Just how free and brave you want to
be? (....) (....) Looky...

Mommas and the babies, they're all
lining up to give the Donald
hugs (....) (....) Looky...
Mommas and the babies, they're all
lining up to give the Donald
hugs. (....) But they'll
have to wait in the back of the line
behind Putin and the Russian
thugs. (....) (....) Hey

Donald is taking off his (....)
Make America Great Again
Hat (....) (....) Hey
Donald is taking off his (....)
Make America Great Again
hat (....) (....) he's
trying on an orange jumpsuit -
he looks much better in
thaaaaaat!

Howl

… and they got so good at lying
that light could not
penetrate the darkness
and the Word became
a long meaningless *howl*
because even lies have no meaning
without truth;
and though all spoke the same language
none did
and words became fists
and everyone lurked
waiting to pounce
lifting their prey
offering

a long meaningless *howl*.

pulling the cat's tale

I can't stream the news today –
all the screens scream howling cats

Republicans dance like bank robbers
Democrats arrange deck chairs on the Titanic

Antarctica is hotter than L.A.
chunk by chunk Greenland slips in the sea

preachers play whack-a-mole with the devil
oligarchs build riot bunkers with wine cellars

voting machines are replaced by Wheel of Fortune
all the answers on Jeopardy are lies

plagues cue up to carry us away
bundled in death, the ironic rescue helicopter

I stick my fingers in my ears, shut my eyes
I stick a needle in my arm, pray for a saucer of milk

A Dream, in Which the Title is Censored

My chest is the canyon where snipers perch
behind the rocks and wait for – what?
Villagers below tend their fires and walk
cozy cobblestone streets
                              Rutabaga
rutabaga I can't make out the words just
a rumble of domestic purring and sniper
fingers slowly uncoil but stay trigger-ready
moist skin rubbing polished metal
ever so delicately, fingers tumescent
pupils dilated
                    Schoolhouse doors open for
recess and children spill out like foam from a
bottle of champagne, unpremeditated bubbles
bursting with shouts and laughter, rolling hoops
and tossing balls and circling the maypole, making
snipers envious and angry
                              Hooves pound
the ground all around, gathering attention
into a bouquet: Behold! It's Genghis Khan
on the precipice, silhouette against orange
sky neither dawn nor dusk
                              looking down at

the valley, a hawk watching a squirrel

                                    and

suddenly I stand on cobblestone streets with the
children rolling their hoops and the couples strolling
arm in arm

                and we hear thunder and see snipers
gallop down the mountainside, waving their
weapons in ecstasy, hissing

   women and children first

MAGA

orange sneer   Fox News
black baby   future thug
brown baby   even worse
national   emergency
"Need wall!"   "Nuh-uh!"
shut down   government
"I win   you lose!"
vigilantes   grab guns
smash grab   all gone
oceans rise   cities burn
Jesus comes   wasn't Jesus
pledge allegiance   martial law
thought police   round up
new home   barbed wire
slave labor   death wish
on knees   pretty please

Breaking News

Tell the truth and shame the

devil?

    Fox News is the

father of lies, mentor of

mental illness, leader of

lynch mobs.

A dangerous buffoon destroys

the world.

      A jailer with a right

tight Jesus grin is waiting

in the wings. The devil's not

ashamed!

Angels with stretchers

carried

    truth

       away.

There *was* a cursory

investigation but the outline of

the body

    chalked

       on

          cement

fades, forgotten, and hell

is raised, and doors

close.

God the Day Drinker

God's the kind of guy you want to have a pint with.
I always perch on the stool beside Him.
"I'll have what He's having!" I say to the bartender.
God thinks that's pretty funny.

Don't believe that 'Word of God' stuff.
He's not a talker. Mention politics
and He throws a shoe at Fox News.
Bring up religion and He starts ordering shots.

Used to, I'd visit the bar but wouldn't see Him.
These days, He's there till closing time.
I heard He was downsized, or on disability,
and that's why no one runs things anymore.

Recently, He switched from beer to martinis.
He's fond of the olives, they're salty, like tears.
I hear He's ordering a round for everyone
but without instructions for an Ark.

A-poc-poc-pocalypse

How will it be when the end settles in?
Will eyes scrutinize
                  recognize
who's a friend and who's just stealing our corn?

Or will the notion of friend be forgotten fashion
goofy bell-bottom britches replaced by
alliances in a game of Survivor
                        where
the Island disappears with the money

Will Jesus come in camouflage with an AK-47
like Pat Robertson dreamed
                     how will we tell
one Jesus from another Jesus
with so many department store
                  Santa Clauses
opening empty boxes?

When we can't say things will get better
what will we say instead?

As the earth tilts, will we keep our balance
by leaning and leaning

                              more to the right
until we're flat on the ground?

Will the new dark age be a bright desert sun
that never quite

                    burns us up
or will a flood waterboard us
and though drowning

                              we'll never die?
Do we get to pick?

Will yowling pulled-tail cats
be mood music

                    when wings are clipped
and we rooster-prance
scratch at memory

                              and peck
our own shit?

How will it be when the end settles in?
Will we grieve our lives

                              or blame
the Creator

                    as if there's a difference?

Everybody Knows

The heaving of the coffeemaker
sounds like Darth Vader
crooking his finger from the dark side
I'm halfway there
because every fried egg's bottom
burns in bacon grease
even sunny-side up

The first day of school, drizzling gray
Heroin dealers in yellow raincoats
wait at bus stops with umbrellas
The bus passes school and keeps going
takes the ramp to the interstate
Some of the children cry
Some ask the man to drive faster

The feed on my phone says
"Eyewitness Commits Suicide"
The attorney general nods
makes the sign of the cross
No one wants to be Mel Gibson
in that movie where
the conspiracy theorist is right

Facebook, Instagram, digital bricks
in a wall to contain the dark side
Swiping left, swiping right
windshield wipers in driving rain
driving to the scene of the crash
the spatula sliding under the egg
preparing to flip it over

Conversion Therapy Song

God doesn't judge you the way people do
a secret that men can't abide
and if you suggest this idea might be true
they'll beat it right out of your hide

God doesn't make you kiss butt to be saved
or punish if you make a flub
All of the membership fees have been waived –
everyone's part of the club

God's not obsessed with your hoo-hahs and weenies
the way they are on church TVs
Be Dick or be Jane or be some in-betweenie
or nothing at all, if you please

It's not about prophets, it's all about profits
that power to loose and to bind
they scribbled that in for the thrill they get off it –
the power to kick your behind

God doesn't judge you the way people do
a secret that men won't abide
and if you suggest this idea might be true
they'll beat it right out of your hide

Happy New Year from Fox & Friends!

Uncork the hard stuff, make faith blind enough!
It's midnight and America's flat on the floor
Hopeless, smeared in the war paint of tears.

Uncork the hard stuff, make faith blind enough!
Rich people drown facts in bathtubs lest they
grow legs and buy guns and commit regicide.

Uncork the hard stuff, make faith blind enough!
Tie America's hands behind her back
Goad her to the gallows with lies.

November 2, 2018

Stepping cautiously in 5 a.m. darkness
hunting a shape I'll recognize as
a rolled-up newspaper, soundless scribbles
less violent than voices on cable news.
On porches of houses still asleep
pumpkins recall innocent witches
holding hands with parents supervising
terror as play that ends in a treat.
A séance of campaign signs haunt lawns
indistinct goblins unreadable in the dark
a troop of mushrooms that might be poisonous
menace with a mind of its own.
Sometimes we see things as they are
before the avalanche of sunrise buries us.

Optics

My horoscope for tomorrow says
I'll take off my rose-colored glasses
be analytical about circumstances
mind my P's and tame my Q's
and be sure not to double-cross the T's
when I sneak past Billy Goat Gruff
to dot my I's
                       as if I don't see
fate feasting on feckless fools
Trump presiding while the rich eat the rest
religions hauling their covenant arks
to high ground and mounting them with artillery.

Don't begrudge me my glasses:
this darkness blinds wherever I open my eyes.

America's Head Spins Like the Girl in The Exorcist

Lifelong obstructer of justice

unindicted felony co-conspirator

four-time bankrupt financial genius

alleged money launderer for the Russian mob

dressing room voyeur at Miss Teen USA

licensed to grab every woman's pussy

creator of a scam charity stealing money

creator of a scam university stealing money

reality show host training America to grovel

fearmonger walling off white from brown

buffoon, blowhard, schoolyard bully

bestower of permission to hate

flaming orange sociopath, Father of Lies

President of the United States of America

Hope

Kent State II but
lock and load with kisses,
hollowpoints opening into flowers

3D guns can't
kill kings of kindness
un-throne queens of moonlit love.

Dear rabid dogs
the new vet can cure you
the new world is a no-kill shelter

madness's vapid vape
dissipates in etheric sky
in a universe bigger than physical eyes see.

Our whirling lassos
will latch round your ankle
tenderly tighten a noose of safe hands.

This evening, a meeting,
me and my team of angels
plotting salvation – it's what we do.

The New Pledge

I pledge allegiance to what's left

of the United States of America

and to the oligarchy that took it in hand,

one delusion (under water)

of selfishness, with nothing for nobody.

Stars and Stripes

The choir performs Kate Smith's version of God
Bless America, alternating red and white stripes
of chorus and solo
                          Carol Burnett's turn, she goes off
script, singing the Emperor is buck-naked

                                              pointing

No one can believe she's doing this but
who can stop singing in the middle of a song?

                                              now

It's out there
what are they going to do
                          kill her?
                          kill her?
                          kill her?
The mic has echo

Whip's lash leaves red and white stripes
over the course of centuries people see

          stars

Night Watch

late at night

    I smell hell

        over the next hill

to the west

        an orange horizon

California in flames

people clutch photographs

    all of us immigrants

    lost in a desert

to the south

        chains rattle

chains in everyone's hands

from the north

                        arctic wind

breath of God's indifference

I stand in the east

on a foggy riverbank

            silhouettes emerge

            ships approach shore

I search for the face of a friend

He Invades My Dreams, Poland is Next

I sit in a tiny newsroom, not quite an
editor, just important enough to make a
mistake
      he's there with us, our guest
giving an interview, but nothing he says
makes sense
          everyone raises an eyebrow
at me, there's no handle I can grab
no pivot point for a lever
              he's wearing his
famous hat but I see only the visor;
the crown is blurred as if there's been
wardrobe malfunction – I figure my clever
editors are denying him opportunity
for propaganda

        then he stands and I
realize he's only been patronizing

                                    he towers

filling the room with his winter

                                    his chest

swells and he sings like a Viking

                                    I can't catch

the words – just "wall" and "ice" – this song
of war in four quatrains about a hammer that
lives to pound

                        he turns around, shows us his

back

    I understand: it wasn't us who obscured
the crown, the secret one he always wore to
hide what is more horrible than we imagine

Measure for Measure

Time is thinking triplets,
triple beats breaking Bastille,
and I'd always thought I was a couplet man

Little Hitlers
goose-step for Trump
but me and my friends are dancing a waltz

Behind the madness
something is happening
angels quitting their day jobs, starting a band

Constitutional Crisis

Did we dream them or did they dream us?

　　pussy-grabbing president

　　　angry red hats

It's easy to imagine the Emperor clothed

　　just close your eyes

　　　lock and load

But it's all going to turn out well, right?

　　　Sure

Inhale　　　　　Exhale

　　Salute

Acknowledgements

Thanks to Sherry Chandler, Katerina Stoykova, Jeff Worley, and others who taught me, my writer pals (you know who you are), Erin Chandler and Brooke Lee for putting the book together, my wife, family, and friends who support me, and Jane Gentry Vance for opening the door of poetry for me.

Mike Wilson's work has appeared in magazines including *Cagibi Literary Journal*, *Stoneboat*, *The Aurorean*, *The Ocotillo Review*, *London Reader*, and in anthologies including *for a better world 2020* and *Anthology of Appalachian Writers Vol. X*. He received Kentucky State Poetry Society's Chaffin/Kash Prize in 2019. He resides in Lexington, Kentucky, but summers in Ecstasy and winters in Despair.

CPSIA information can be obtained
at www.ICGtesting.com
Printed in the USA
LVHW090310090720
660097LV00007B/632